Celebrate
Christian Festivals

Series editor: Jan Thompson

Jan Thompson

Heinemann

First published in Great Britain by
Heinemann Publishers (Oxford) Ltd
Halley Court, Jordan Hill, Oxford OX2 8EJ

MADRID ATHENS PARIS FLORENCE PRAGUE
WARSAW PORTSMOUTH NH CHICAGO
SAO PAULO SINGAPORE TOKYO MELBOURNE
AUCKLAND IBADAN GABORONE
JOHANNESBURG

Designed by Visual Image Ltd
Colour reproduction by Track QSP

Printed in Hong Kong / China

99
10 9 8 7 6 5 4

ISBN 0 431 06958 1

This title is also available in a hardback library edition
(ISBN 0 431 06947 6)

British Library Cataloguing in Publication Data
Thompson, Jan
   Christian Festivals. – (Celebrate Series)
   I. Title II. Series
   263.9

Acknowledgements
The Publishers would like to thank the following for
permission to reproduce photographs.

Popperfoto: p.4; Jan Thompson: p.5; Jan Thompson: p.6;
Ace Photo Agency/Michael Bluestone: p.6; Jan Thompson:
p.8; Robert Harding Picture Library: p.10; Ace Photo Agency:
p.11; The Children's Society: p.12; Christ Bowler/Abbey
Studios: p.13; Jan Thompson: p.14; Jan Thompson: p.15;
Jan Thompson: p.16; Zefa Pictures: p.16; Barry Lewis/
Network Photographers: p.17; Jan Thompson: p.18;
Jan Thompson: p.19; Zefa Pictures: p.20; Topham Picturepoint:
p.21; Royal Mail 1994, designed by Yvonne Gilbert: p.22;
Britstock-IFA Ltd: p.23; Frank Spooner Pictures: p.24;
Tony Morrison/South American Pictures: p.25;
Jan Thompson: p.26; Stuart Franklin, Pizarro/Magnum Photos:
P.27; Abbas/Magnum Photos: p.28; Vika/Impact Photos: p.29;
Jan Thompson: p.30; Sonia Halliday Photographs: p.31;
Jan Thompson: p.32; Caroline Penn/Impact Photos;
Homer Sykes/Impact Photos: p.34; Andes Press Agency: p.34;
Keith Ellis: P.35; The Bridgeman Art Library: p.36;
Mike Williams/Mary Glasgow Publications: p.37;
Jan Thompson: p.38; St Botolph's Project: p.39;
Cosmos/Impact Photos: p.40; Telegraph Colour Library: p.41;
Sonia Halliday Photographs: p.42; Frank Spooner Pictures:
p.43

Cover photograph Zefa Pictures

Details of written sources
Christingle hymn, Come and Praise 1, No.29, BBC
Publications: p.13; Carol, Hymns Ancient and Modern
Revised, No.432, Hymns Ancient and Modern Ltd: p.17;
Harvest song, Hymns Ancient and Modern Revised, No.483,
Hymns Ancient and Modern Ltd: p.38; Hymn, Hymns Ancient
and Modern Revised, No.525, Hymns Ancient and Modern
Ltd: p.43; Acts 2:1-4, Good News Bible, The Bible Societies
and Collins, a division of Harper Collins: p.36

Our thanks to Denise Cush of Bath College of Further
Education for her comments in the preparation of this
book.

Every effort has been made to contact copyright holders
of any material reproduced in this book. Any omissions will
be rectified in subsequent printings if notice is given to the
Publisher.

Contents

Introduction

This unit tells you who Christians are and what they believe.

*Each year at the festival of Easter thousands of Roman Catholics gather in St Peter's Square in Rome. They wait to see the Pope come out onto his balcony, where he says a prayer over them to **bless** them.*

Christians are people who believe in **God** and follow Jesus Christ. He lived two thousand years ago. Since that time, **Christianity** has become the biggest religion in the world. Christians belong to **churches** where they meet together to worship God. There are many different types of churches. Half the Christians in the world belong to the Roman Catholic Church. This is led by the **Pope** in Rome, which is in Italy. Many Christians in England belong to the Church of England. There are many Protestant churches, like the Methodist Church and the Baptist Church. Many Christians in Eastern Europe belong to Orthodox churches like the Russian Orthodox Church. As Christians have moved to different parts of the world, they have set up their own churches throughout the world.

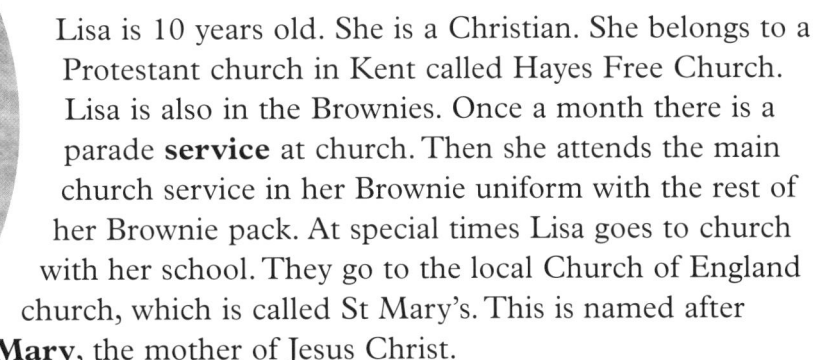

Lisa is 10 years old. She is a Christian. She belongs to a Protestant church in Kent called Hayes Free Church. Lisa is also in the Brownies. Once a month there is a parade **service** at church. Then she attends the main church service in her Brownie uniform with the rest of her Brownie pack. At special times Lisa goes to church with her school. They go to the local Church of England church, which is called St Mary's. This is named after **Mary**, the mother of Jesus Christ.

James and John Greenidge are also 10 years old. As you can see, they are twins. James and John belong to a Christian family. They were named after two of Jesus' best friends, who were also brothers. James and John go to a Roman Catholic church in Kent, called St Joseph's. This is named after Joseph, the husband of Mary. James and John are **altar** boys at their church. This means that they help the **priest** during the service. You can see them here, by the altar in their church, dressed in the special clothes they wear for the service. James and John also go to a Catholic primary school. The priest you see in the photo goes into their school and sometimes leads the worship there.

James and John are altar boys. They help the priest during services.

Festivals

This unit describes the different ways that special events are celebrated.

> **I was 10 on my last birthday. I used to have parties, but now I go out for the day. My birthday's in August and I'm usually on holiday. Last year we went out to the zoo and in the evening we went out for dinner to a posh restaurant. When we got back from holiday, six of my friends came for a sleep-over.**
>
> *– Lisa*

Festivals are happy times which we share with family and friends. Often there are presents and cards and lots of nice things to eat. We celebrate together to remember important events. We remember birthdays and anniversaries.

Children celebrating at a birthday party.

Religious festivals

Religions also have festivals to remember important events. **Christians** have lots of festivals. Many of these festivals remind them of important events in the life of Jesus Christ. His birth is remembered at **Christmas** and his death at **Easter**. Some festivals celebrate important events in the history of the **church**, like the birthday of the church at **Pentecost**. Saints' Days recall the lives of special Christians.

People remember important events from long ago because this helps them to think about their own lives now. For instance, when Christians remember that Jesus was born among poor people, it reminds them to help poor people today.

The Christian year

Look at the Christian calendar. You will notice that it starts in December, not January, and each section cuts across our months of the year. The church's year is based on its main festivals of Christmas, Easter and Pentecost.

ADVENT is the time when Christians prepare for Christmas.
CHRISTMAS celebrates the birth of Jesus Christ.
EPIPHANY remembers the story of the Wise Men, who found Jesus when he was still a toddler.
LENT is when Christians prepare for Easter.
EASTER remembers the death and **resurrection** of Jesus Christ.
ASCENSION is the story of Jesus going to **heaven**.
PENTECOST marks the coming of the Holy Spirit to the first Christians, and the beginning of the church.

Calendar colours

The church uses different colours for different times of the year. Purple is for the serious, thinking times. White is for happy festivals. Red is for Pentecost or Whit **Sunday**, to stand for the fire of the Holy Spirit. Red is also used on Saints' Days, for the blood of those who died for their **faith**. Green is used in the weeks after Pentecost. It is the colour of growth, when Christians should be growing in their faith.

This book will tell you about some of the Christian festivals. It will tell you about some of the ways Christians celebrate them. It will also help you to understand why they are important for Christians today, even when they are remembering events from long ago.

A diagram of the Christian calendar.

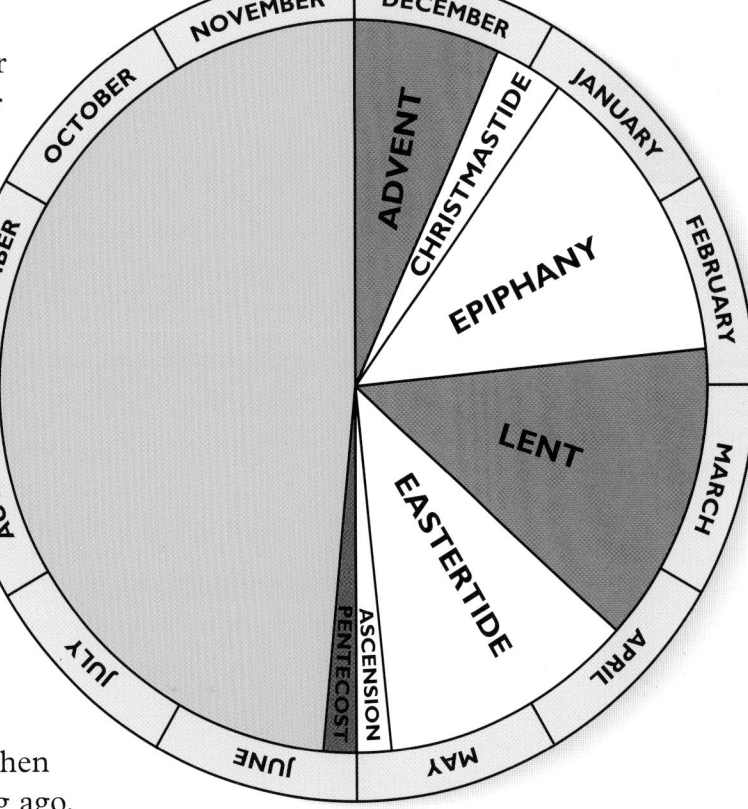

Advent

This unit describes how Christians celebrate Advent, the beginning of their church year.

> **I normally get an Advent calendar with chocolates in. I have one and my little brother Nathan has one. We keep them in the kitchen. We keep them out of Nathan's reach because last year he opened all the windows in one day. We're supposed to open one a day. It's like a countdown for Christmas.**
>
> *– Lisa*

An Advent ring.

When is Advent?

Advent is the beginning of the church's year. It might seem strange to have a new year in December, when 1 January is New Year's Day. But then, we have other new years at different times. For example, the new school year starts in September.

Advent **Sunday** is the Sunday nearest to St Andrew's Day on 30 November. Sometimes it comes just before St Andrew's Day, and sometimes just after. This is the beginning of Advent. It lasts right through December until Christmas Day on the 25th.

Making preparations

Advent is a time when **Christians** prepare themselves for Christmas. This does not just mean buying presents and food. They prepare themselves by reading the **Bible** and **praying**, at **church** and at home. They think about the difference Jesus made by coming into the world. They make a special effort to live the way Jesus taught people to live.

Counting the days

Many churches use an Advent ring. This is a ring of holly with four coloured candles round the edge and one big white candle in the middle. On Advent Sunday, one coloured candle is lit at the beginning of the church **service**. On the next Sunday, two candles are lit. This happens on each of the four Sundays in Advent until all four coloured candles are lit. On Christmas Day the big white candle is also lit. This stands for Jesus Christ, who is called the Light of the World. Christians use this symbol for Jesus Christ because they believe he brightened up the world by bringing goodness and hope.

Some Christians have an Advent candle in their homes. This is a big candle marked off for 24 days. On each day of December the candle is lit for about half an hour until it burns down to the next date. The candle lasts until Christmas Day.

The Advent calendar, the Advent ring and the Advent candle are all ways of counting off the days until Christmas. Christmas is such an important festival that Christians look forward to it right through the four weeks of Advent.

An Advent candle.

The Scottish flag.

St Andrew

St Andrew was one of the earliest followers of Jesus. He was one of his 12 **disciples**. He was a fisherman from Galilee, the brother of Simon-Peter. St Andrew is the **patron saint** of Scotland. The Scottish flag has the X-shaped cross of St Andrew on it. St Andrew's Day is 30 November.

St Lucia's Day

This unit tells you how people in Sweden celebrate St Lucia's Day.

> **It was my little sister's turn to be St Lucia this year. Elsa is only 4 years old, so Mum helped us. She only lit the candles for a little while. She was afraid Elsa would get burnt.**
>
> *– Britt*

St Lucia buns.

St Lucia buns

St Lucia buns are made from sweet bread dough with a few raisins in it. They are coloured yellow with saffron. Once upon a time saffron was a very expensive spice. It was hard to get hold of, so it was only used on very special occasions. The bread dough is pulled into different shapes before it is baked.

Swedish girl dressed as St Lucia.

What happens on St Lucia's Day

St Lucia's Day is 13 December. In Sweden this is like the beginning of **Christmas**. It is celebrated everywhere: in schools, **churches**, shops and offices. They have processions where the main girl is dressed as a Lucia queen or bride. She dresses in a long white dress and a red sash. On her head is a crown of evergreen leaves and lighted candles. Other girls also dress in white and hold a candle each. The boys are called 'star boys', and they wear cone-shaped hats made from thin cardboard and decorated with paper stars. They all sing special **carols** and give out ginger biscuits. In some churches the choir dresses up for the procession. After the carols, everyone goes to the church hall for coffee and buns.

In Swedish homes it is often the youngest girl who dresses up as St Lucia. She is supposed to make breakfast in bed for the rest of the family. They all enjoy coffee and yellow St Lucia buns.

Who was St Lucia?

We do not know much about St Lucia. She was an early **Christian martyr**. This means that she died because of her religion. The white dress may stand for her holiness, and the red sash for her death. Many legends have grown up about her. One is that she helped the Christians who were hiding in the tunnels under Rome in Italy. She found her way through the dark tunnels by wearing candles on her head, a bit like a miner's torch. Another legend says that at a time of great hunger in Sweden she miraculously appeared and fed people.

Light and decorations

St Lucia is the **patron saint** of light, so people celebrate her day by lighting candles. Her saint's day comes in the middle of winter. December is the darkest month of the year in Sweden. Even before the time of Jesus, people celebrated mid-winter festivals with light. They wanted to brighten up the long dark days. They also decorated their homes with evergreens, like holly and fir trees. These things were living when everything else in nature seemed to be dead. They gave them hope that spring would come again with lighter days, and everything would start growing again. Some of these old customs have now become part of Christmas celebrations. There are lots of different lights at Christmas, and people decorate their homes with trees and holly. You will find other Christian customs that started before **Christianity**. Often they have been given new Christian meanings.

Christmas evergreen tree indoors, lit up with candles.

Christingle

This unit tells you about Christingle services that celebrate God and the world.

> **At the Christingle service we have oranges and there are sweets stuck into them on sticks. We don't eat the sweets at the service, but we eat them afterwards. The lights are switched off so that the church is dark when the candles in the oranges are lit.**
>
> *– John*

The **Christingle** is a **Christian** symbol of God's gifts to the world.

- The orange stands for the world that **God** has created.
- The four cocktail sticks stand for the four seasons of the year.
- The fruit, nuts and sweets stand for the fruits of the earth.
- The red ribbon stands for God's love in sending Jesus to the earth.
- The candle stands for Jesus Christ, the Light of the World.
- The word 'Christingle' means 'Christ-light.'

This picture from The Children's Society shows a Christingle.

The history of Christingle

The first Christingle **service** was held in Germany in 1747. The **minister** gave the children Christingles to take home, and told them to put them in their windows. This would remind people that Jesus was the Light of the World. Over 200 years later, in 1968, Christingle was started in England by The Children's Society.

Children with lighted Christingles at a Christingle service.

Christingle today

Christingle services are now enjoyed by thousands of people, mainly children, every year. They have songs, readings and prayers on the theme of light. Money is collected at these services for the work of the Children's Society. This **charity** belongs to the Church of England. It helps children in need.

A Christingle service is usually held around **Christmas** time. As this is darkest winter in the northern hemisphere, it is a good time for Christians to think of Jesus as the Light of the World. Also, the service is to thank God for his gifts. Christians believe that God's greatest gift was Jesus himself.

A Christingle hymn

This is the chorus and one verse from a Christian **hymn** on the theme of light. This might be sung at a Christingle service.

'From the darkness came light,
from the blackest of nights.
Wait for the morning, the sunlight,
the dawning.
From the darkness came light.

Jesus was born in a stall,
born to bring light to us all.
He came to love us,
a new life to give us;
Jesus was born in a stall.'

Christmas Crib Service

This unit tells you how cribs are made
to remind people of the birth of Jesus.

Middle Eastern shepherds grazing
their sheep. They still find shelter in
caves in the hills. Jesus was probably
born in such a cave.

In the **Bible** there are two accounts of the birth of
Jesus. There is one in St Matthew's **Gospel** and one
in St Luke's Gospel. Luke tells us that Jesus was
born in a stable in **Bethlehem**, and that shepherds
came to visit him on that first **Christmas** night.

Christmas cribs

A Christmas crib is a model of the stable where
Jesus was born. It has the figures of **Mary** and
Joseph, the baby Jesus laid in a manger and some
shepherds. It also has model animals like sheep, a
donkey and cattle. The custom started with St
Francis of Assisi nearly 800 years ago. One
Christmas Eve he re-created a life-size scene of
Jesus' birth in a cave for the villagers nearby. They
found that it helped them to imagine what the first
Christmas must have been like. The idea spread
from Italy, but with smaller models instead.

Blessing the crib

Christmas cribs are set up in many **churches**, to remind people of the story of Jesus' birth. There is a special **service** for the **priest** to **bless** the crib. Here are some words from the prayers that the priest might use:

'Bless this crib which we have prepared to celebrate that **holy** birth. May all who see it be strengthened in **faith**.'

This girl is kneeling in front of a Christmas crib. Some of the characters from the Nativity are missing – the Wise Men. We hear about the wise men in St Matthew's Gospel. These are added to the crib after Christmas, at the festival of **Epiphany***. This is when the Wise Men are remembered by the church.*

Mince pies

Mince pies are eaten at Christmas. They are round pastry cases, filled with sweet mincemeat and covered with a pastry lid. Originally they were not round but oval in shape. The mincemeat really was meat. They had no lids, but a small piece of pastry was laid across the top. This was meant to look like a tiny cradle for the baby Jesus.

Do you help to make the mince pies at home? Try making some oval ones, half-covered with pastry – like a cradle.

Carols

> **I go with my school to St Mary's Church for the carol service. It's in the afternoon and we go home afterwards. Normally we have a Nativity play. That tells the story of Jesus' birth. The mums and dads watch. They put the words of the carols up on a screen so that they can sing them.**
>
> *– Lisa*

Carols are religious pop songs. Unlike most church music, carols are the simple, popular songs of ordinary people. Most are **Christmas** carols, telling the stories and beliefs about Christmas. Many carols are hundreds of years old. Others are new. They often have a dance rhythm to them, which is not surprising because the word 'carol' originally meant 'to dance in a ring'.

Carol singers collecting money.

Where to hear carols

Carols can be heard almost everywhere at Christmas time. They are played in shops and on the radio. They are sung in schools and in churches. People go out carol-singing in groups. You may see them at busy places like supermarkets. Or they may come knocking on your door. Often they collect money at the same time for a **charity**.

On the afternoon of Christmas Eve, there is a special carol service on television. This comes from the beautiful **chapel** of King's College at Cambridge University. This Service of Nine Lessons and Carols started there over 75 years ago. Many other churches now use the same service. The lessons are readings from the **Bible**, the **Christian holy** book. They were chosen to tell the story of **God's** love for the world, ending with the story of Jesus' birth. Carols are sung between each reading.

The carols

This grand service always starts with one choirboy singing a solo. He sings the first verse of the carol 'Once in Royal David's City.' Several choirboys are prepared for this, and the boy who is chosen is only told just before the service! Imagine what a great honour this is for him.

Some verses from 'Once in Royal David's City' follow. 'Royal David's City' is Bethlehem. It was here that King **David** of the Bible was born. Jesus was also born here. Notice the Christian beliefs about Jesus as God, Lord and Saviour. Notice also the beliefs that when Christians die they will be with him in **heaven**.

A carol

*Once in royal David's city
stood a lowly cattle shed,
where a mother laid her baby
in a manger for his bed:
Mary was that mother mild,
Jesus Christ her little child.*

*He came down to earth from heaven
who is God and Lord of all,
and his shelter was a stable,
and his cradle was a stall;
with the poor and mean and lowly
lived on earth our Saviour holy.*

*Not in that poor lowly stable,
with the oxen standing by,
we shall see him; but in heaven,
set at God's right hand on high;
where like stars his children crowned
all in white shall wait around.*

Choir boys at the carol service from King's College, Cambridge.

Christmas Eve

This unit explains how some people celebrate the day before Christmas Day, when Jesus was born.

" **We've only been once to Midnight Mass. I thought it was going to be good at first, going to church in the middle of the night. But it was a very long Mass and I just felt tired. I was serving at the altar and I nearly fell asleep.** "

– John

Midnight Mass

Mass is a special church **service** where bread and wine are used to stand for the body and blood of Jesus. **Christians** feel very close to Jesus when they eat and drink the bread and wine. Many churches hold a service of Midnight Mass on **Christmas** Eve. This is because Christians want to feel specially close to Jesus on the night when they remember his birth.

Christmas pilgrims

A **pilgrim** is a religious person who travels to a **holy** place. Many Christians travel to Israel at **Christmas** time. They crowd into Manger Square in **Bethlehem** on Christmas Eve. This is outside the Church of the **Nativity**. The famous bells here ring out at midnight and are shown on televisions around the world. Christian pilgrims to Bethlehem can go down some steps into a cave under the church. In the floor is a star marking the place where it is believed Jesus was born. It is a custom for the pilgrims to kneel down and kiss the star.

Pilgrims can also visit shepherds' caves around Bethlehem. This gives them a better idea of the type of place where Jesus was born, for these caves have always been used to keep animals in.

The story of Jesus' birth

Luke's **Gospel** tells us that **Mary** and her husband Joseph travelled south to Bethlehem to register for the Roman taxes. Mary was pregnant at the time. She had been told by an **angel** that her son would be the Christ, the long-awaited **Saviour**. No sooner had they arrived in Bethlehem, than Mary felt her baby coming. But Bethlehem was packed with travellers, and they could not find anywhere to stay. In the end, they had to make do with a stable. They made a cot for the new-born baby out of the animals' feeding trough, called a manger. The story goes that there were shepherds out on the hills looking after their sheep. Suddenly an angel appeared to them. He told them that the Saviour had been born and was lying in a manger. The shepherds set off to find him.

This story teaches Christians about **God**. They might have expected their Lord to be born in luxury, not a stable. They might have expected kings to be told of his birth, not ordinary shepherds on night-shift. This teaches Christians that God knows what it is like to be poor, and he cares for ordinary people. It teaches Christians that they, too, must care for the poor and needy.

The star on the floor in the cave under the church in Bethlehem where Jesus is supposed to have been born.

Christmas Day

This unit describes how people celebrate Jesus' birth on Christmas Day.

> **Last year Nathan woke me up at 1 o'clock in the morning. He wanted to open his presents, but I said it was too early. We woke up again at about 7 o'clock. We had presents in our pillow-case from Father Christmas.**
>
> *– Lisa*

A child on Christmas morning.

Christmas card showing a dove – a symbol of peace.

The Christmas tradition

Christmas is a very popular festival. It is usually a family occasion. **Christians** are celebrating the birth of Jesus their **Saviour**, and they want to share their happiness with others. It is especially popular with children, who get lots of presents. It was traditional to leave out socks or stockings to be filled with presents. You can now buy special Christmas stockings for this. There are different traditions about who brings the presents. In Germany, it is said to be the child Jesus. British children say that Father Christmas comes down the chimney with their presents. American children call him Santa Claus. In Austria and Czechoslovakia it is said to be Saint Nicholas.

Christmas Day in church

Churches usually have **services** on Christmas morning. Everyone wishes each other 'Happy Christmas' as they go in. They sing Christmas **carols** instead of the usual **hymns**. The collection on Christmas Day is often given to a **charity**, to help people in need. People are usually very generous because they want to say 'thank you' to **God** for all the good things they enjoy at Christmas.

Christmas cards

Apart from presents, people also send each other Christmas cards. This custom started about a hundred years ago, and it is now very popular. Cards are a way of keeping in touch with friends and family, and of wishing people a merry Christmas, and a happy New Year. There are many different designs on Christmas cards. Some are winter scenes; some show presents and Christmas dinners. Many Christians like to send cards which show the religious meaning of Christmas. They might show the birth of Jesus, or they might have a symbol on them. The dove, for example, is a symbol of peace. Christians believe that Jesus was born to bring peace on earth.

St Nicholas

*Little is known about St Nicholas, who was an early **bishop** of the Church. The famous legend about him tells how he saved three girls who were so poor that they could not afford to marry. At night, he secretly left them three bags of gold. St Nicholas is the **patron saint** of children, and is supposed to bring them presents. 'Santa Claus' is another name for St Nicholas.*

Why is Christmas in December?

Christmas is celebrated every year on 25 December, but no-one knows exactly when Jesus was born. The church chose this date over 300 years after his birth. Darkest winter is a good time for Christians to celebrate the birth of Jesus, who is known as the Light of the World, and Christians find that Jesus gives them hope at the darkest, saddest times in their lives.

Of course, when Christians settled in the southern hemisphere, Christmas came in the summer. Many Australians have a Christmas barbecue on the beach and hold open-air Christmas processions.

An open-air Christmas procession in Australia.

Epiphany

This unit tells you about the Wise Men who came to see the baby Jesus, and who are remembered on Epiphany every year.

> **Epiphany is on 6th January and it's when the Wise Men came to see Jesus. We have the Wise Men in our school Nativity play, which is performed in church. They come up the centre of the church, then we all sing the carol 'We three kings.'**

Where the Wise Men are described

There are two nativity stories in the **Bible**. Luke's **Gospel** tells the story of the **angels**, the shepherds and Jesus born in a stable. The story of the Wise Men comes from St Matthew's Gospel. The two stories are usually joined together in school Nativity plays, but the church keeps them separate. The story of the wise men is celebrated in church 12 days after **Christmas**, at **Epiphany**. This is a Greek word which means 'to make known.' **Christians** are happy that Jesus was made known to other people, as well as to the Jews.

Children dressed as the Wise Men on a British Christmas stamp, 1994.

The Wise Men's gifts

The gifts of the Wise Men are important. Each was a symbol which teaches Christians about Jesus. Gold was for a king; and Christians call Jesus the King of Kings. Frankincense was used in worship; and Christians worship Jesus Christ. Myrrh was a perfume which was put on dead bodies; and Jesus was to die. For the past 700 years these three gifts have been presented at the **altar** of the **Chapel** Royal in St James' Palace in London by a member of the British royal family. In Spain, Epiphany is when children get lots of presents, rather than at Christmas. They write letters to the Three Kings to tell them what they would like. There are big processions, with three men dressed up as the kings.

Spanish Twelfth Night celebrations. Christians think of the Wise Men as three kings.

The story of the Wise Men

*Soon after Jesus was born, some Wise Men arrived in **Jerusalem**. They had come from the east because they had seen a special star. It meant that a new king was born. They asked at King Herod's palace in Jerusalem, but Herod knew nothing of a new king, and he was worried by the news. Who was this new king? Would he grow up to take his throne? There was a passage in the Bible which said that a leader of the Jews would come from **Bethlehem**. So Herod sent the Wise Men to the little town of Bethlehem, a few miles south of Jerusalem. He asked them to tell him if they found the king, so that he could come and worship him too. In fact, all he wanted to do was to kill this new king, because he saw him as a threat. When the Wise Men found the child Jesus in Bethlehem, they worshipped him and gave him their presents of gold, frankincense and myrrh. They did not tell Herod. They had been warned in a dream, and went home another way. Herod was so angry that he sent his soldiers to Bethlehem to kill all the boys under the age of two. But he did not kill Jesus. **Mary** and Joseph had already taken him to Egypt, where they stayed until Herod's death.*

Lent

This unit is about the 40 days before Easter known as Lent.

> **We have a special Mass on Ash Wednesday. You have to go up to the front of the church and Father just dips his hand in a bowl of ashes and puts a cross on your forehead.**
>
> – *John*

> **Ash Wednesday is the beginning of Lent. We give up sweets during Lent. Well, I say I do, but I can't!**
>
> – *James*

What is Lent?

Lent is kept by many churches. It is a time of 40 days before **Easter** (not counting **Sundays**). Its name simply refers to the time of year when the days begin to lengthen with the coming of spring. It starts with Ash Wednesday. Ashes are a sign of being sorry. Lent is a time when **Christians** prepare for Easter by thinking about the things they have done wrong. We all make mistakes, we sometimes hurt other people, and we can feel disappointed with ourselves. Christians believe that **God** forgives their sins and gives them a fresh start if they are really sorry.

Giving things up for Lent

Christians used to **fast** during Lent, which means giving up some food. They did this because Jesus spent 40 days in the desert without food. Some Christians still give up things like sweets during Lent. Some try to do something extra for God at this time, like reading the **Bible** every day, or saving for a **charity** in a special Lent box.

A pancake race.

Pancake Day

The day before Lent starts is called **Shrove Tuesday**, because people used to go to church to be 'shriven' on that day. This means they confessed their sins to a **priest** and were forgiven. Shrove Tuesday is also called Pancake Day, or Mardi Gras in France, which means Grease Tuesday. Pancakes were eaten on this day to use up all the rich foods before Lent. Many of us still eat pancakes on Shrove Tuesday and some people run in pancake-races.

Carnivals

Carnivals also take place at this time. The word 'carnival' means 'take away meat', and it was a chance to celebrate together before the serious time of Lent. Carnivals usually have big processions through the streets with decorated floats. The West Indian carnivals make special music with their steel bands.

West Indian carnival.

Mothering Sunday

This comes in the middle of Lent, on the fourth Sunday. Most people now call it 'Mother's Day', but it began as a religious festival. In church, special prayers are said for our mothers, like this one:

'Heavenly Father, we thank you for our mothers. They are very special to us because they gave us birth. Thank you for all the love they have given us. Thank you for all their hard work in bringing us up. Help us always to love them in return. Amen.'

Some churches have little bunches of spring flowers for the children to give to their mothers.

Palm Sunday

This unit tells you how people celebrate the day that Jesus came to Jerusalem.

> **The priest carries a big palm branch in church on Palm Sunday. And he gives you a palm cross. That was to remember when Jesus came to Jerusalem and they chopped down palms and laid them down for him.**
>
> *– James*

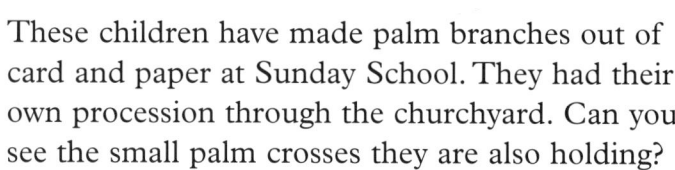

> **Dad's from Barbados and we go every two years. I've seen palm trees there.**
>
> *– John*

These children have made palm branches out of card and paper at Sunday School. They had their own procession through the churchyard. Can you see the small palm crosses they are also holding?

■ *Palm trees.*

What is Palm Sunday?

Palm Sunday celebrates Jesus' arrival at **Jerusalem** for the Jewish festival of Passover. Many people must have hoped that Jesus was the **Saviour** who was promised to them in the **Bible**. This is what they did: 'The next day the large crowd that had come to the Passover Festival heard that Jesus was coming to Jerusalem. So they took branches of palm trees and went out to meet him, shouting, "Praise **God**! God **bless** him who comes in the name of the Lord! God bless the King of Israel."' (John 12:12–13 Good News Bible.)

A Palm Sunday procession in Latin America with a statue of Jesus on a donkey.

Palm Sunday processions

In hot countries, particularly Roman Catholic countries, the Palm Sunday procession often takes place out in the streets. Sometimes a live donkey is used in the procession with a statue of Jesus on it. This is because Jesus rode into Jerusalem on a donkey, to show that he came in peace. If you look at the hair on a donkey's back, you will see that it forms the shape of a cross. Folklore says it has been there ever since Jesus rode into Jerusalem on a donkey, because it was there that he died on a cross.

Palm crosses

Palm Sunday is both a happy and a sad occasion. **Christians** are happy because they are singing Jesus' praises. But they are also sad because they know that Jesus died on a cross less than a week after he had entered Jerusalem. So Christians are given little palm crosses on Palm Sunday, made from single palm leaves. It is the beginning of **Holy Week**, the last week of **Lent**. This is a very special week for Christians, as they read in the Bible about the last few days of Jesus' life. Many churches have **services** every day this week.

The palm-crosses that are left over are kept for almost a year. Then they are burnt up and their ashes are used on **Ash Wednesday** to put on people's foreheads on the first day of Lent.

Maundy Thursday

This unit tells you what happened on the day before Jesus died, and how it is remembered.

> **At the service on Maundy Thursday 12 men go up and have their feet washed. My Dad's usually one of them. The priest washes their feet.**
>
> *– James*

An African priest blesses the bread and wine at Holy Communion.

The Last Supper

On the night before his death, Jesus ate a final meal with his **disciples**. This is called the Last Supper. At that meal, he took the bread and the wine and gave them new meaning. He said that the bread was his body, and the wine was his blood. Jesus must have known that he would soon be taken away from them. He wanted to leave them something to remember him by. Throughout history **Christians** have shared bread and wine together to remember Jesus. It is done at a special **church service**. This has various names such as **Mass**, **Holy Communion** and the Lord's Supper. Not all churches do this, but for those that do, it is their most important service. The Holy Communion service that Christians attend on the Thursday evening in Holy Week is extra special. It is a time to remember how it all began on the night before Jesus died.

What is Maundy Thursday?

The Thursday in Holy Week is called **Maundy Thursday**. 'Maundy' means a mandate or command. St John's **Gospel** records a new command that Jesus gave his followers on this night. It was that they should love one another as he loved them. He showed them how much he loved them by washing their feet. This was the servant's job. By doing it himself, Jesus was teaching his disciples that none of them should be too proud to look after one another.

Sometimes, at the Maundy Thursday service, the priest will wash the feet of 12 people from the church. The **Pope** washes the feet of 12 choirboys in St Peter's cathedral in Rome. In Britain, the monarch no longer washes the feet of 12 poor people, but the Queen gives out special Maundy money to a group of pensioners. Each year the Queen goes to a different cathedral for the special Royal Maundy service, which is shown on television.

Foot-washing is done in Pentecostal churches at other times of year as well. They do it at their **Sunday** service, to show their love for one another. The symbols of bread and wine are also used at other times.

Maundy Thursday evening

After the Last Supper, Jesus went with his disciples to the Garden of Gethsemane on the Mount of Olives. Before the soldiers came to arrest him, he had asked his disciples to stay awake with him while he **prayed**. Today, Christians often remember this by staying in church for an extra hour after the service is over on the evening of Maundy Thursday. Some may stay even longer in silent prayer.

Jesus was kept in prison on Thursday night. The next day, the Jews handed him over to the Roman governor.

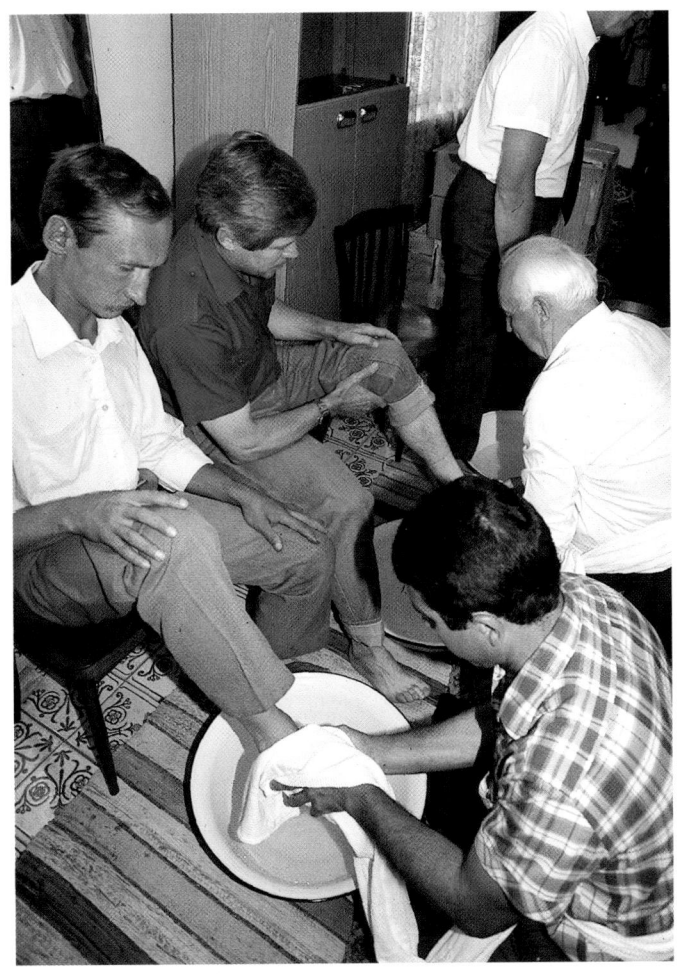

Foot-washing.

Good Friday

This unit tells you how Good Friday recalls the day that Jesus died.

66 At school we sat down and had silence to think about Jesus' death – how he died and why he died. We had paper to write down our ideas. Some people thought the Jewish leaders wanted to kill him because they thought he was telling lies about being God's son. But most of us thought he died because he wanted to die for other people to live. He was caring. 99

– Lisa

The Station of the Cross showing Simon helping Jesus carry the cross.

What is Good Friday?

In many ways, **Good Friday** is not good at all. It is the day when **Christians** remember Jesus' death. It is thought that the name may have started as 'God's Friday' rather than 'Good Friday'.

Hot cross buns.

The Stations of the Cross

In Catholic **churches** you can see 14 pictures, or plaques, around the walls. These are called the **Stations of the Cross**. They tell the story of the final hours of Jesus' life on the first 'Good Friday'. They start with his trial in front of the Roman governor and finish with his burial. They are called 'stations' because this means a stopping place. Each Station of the Cross was a stopping place on Jesus' final journey to his death. They are also stopping places for Catholic Christians to think and **pray** about the meaning of Jesus' suffering. For instance, the fifth Station shows a man called Simon being made to help Jesus carry his cross. Christians might pray for strength to help Jesus whenever they are called upon to do so. Christians believe that they can help Jesus today by helping anyone who is in need, because these were the people that Jesus loved.

Christian **pilgrims** to the **Holy** Land pray at the Stations of the Cross in the Via Dolorosa. This is the winding street along which Jesus carried his cross. Its name means 'Way of Sorrows.' Often, groups of pilgrims carry a life-size cross with them.

The symbol of the cross

The cross has become the main symbol for **Christianity**. It is traditional to eat hot cross buns on Good Friday, to mark the day when Jesus died on the cross. Many Christians wear crosses as jewellery, or have them hanging on their walls. You can usually see crosses both inside and outside church buildings. There are different shapes and types of crosses, all with their own special meanings. A cross with the figure of Jesus on it is called a crucifix. This reminds Christians of Jesus' suffering.

Some Christians go to church on Good Friday morning for a **service** to 'venerate' the cross. This means to show it respect. During this sad service, they come up to the front and kiss the crucifix. From midday until 3 o'clock in the afternoon, Christians remember the time that Jesus hung on the cross. Some churches have a three-hour service at this time.

The Via Dolorosa, the road along which Jesus walked to his death on a cross.

Easter

This unit looks at the important Easter festival, which reminds people of Jesus' death and new life.

> **On Easter Day I watch all the programmes about Jesus on television. I read the Bible – it's a children's Bible. And I draw pictures of Jesus – all the different stories I've heard about him.**
>
> – *Lisa*

> **Normally I get 10 or 12 Easter eggs. I don't eat them all at once!**
>
> – *Lisa*

What is Easter?

Easter is the most important of all the **Christian** festivals. There is a long build-up to it during the six weeks of **Lent**. During the final week, called **Holy** Week, many **churches** hold **services** every day. In Britain there is a four-day public holiday from **Good Friday** to Easter Monday. Easter eggs are given on Easter **Sunday**. Easter parades are a tradition on Bank Holiday Monday, when people wear Easter bonnets.

Easter eggs

Young birds and reptiles hatch from eggs, so Easter eggs are symbols of new life. Also, as they are cracked open, they stand for the empty tomb of Jesus. Orthodox Christians have hard-boiled eggs dyed red, which they crack against each other (a bit like a game of conkers). Other eggs are painted with beautiful patterns.

A bird sitting on its eggs.

The resurrection

Easter is the time when Christians remember that Jesus died on the cross, was buried, and then started a new life. After the sadness of Good Friday, Christians rejoice together as they celebrate their belief in his **resurrection**. Church buildings are bright with spring flowers, and happy songs are sung, with words like these:

> 'Jesus Christ is risen today.
> **Alleluia**.'
> 'Let shouts of praise and joy outburst. Alleluia.'

Why is Easter so important for Christians? Without the resurrection, Jesus would have been seen as a great man. After the resurrection, Christians called Jesus 'my Lord and my **God**.'

Different Easters

Easter can come on any Sunday between 21 March and 25 April. It depends on the full moon at the Jewish Passover festival. Christians found it difficult to agree when to celebrate it. The Western and Eastern Churches still follow a different calendar. Their Easters are sometimes as much as a month apart.

Greek Orthodox Christians gathered in candlelight at midnight on Easter Eve.

Easter is a very big festival in Eastern Orthodox countries like Greece. Late on Holy Saturday night Orthodox Christians gather at church. They will be there to celebrate Christ's resurrection as Easter Day dawns. Just before midnight they go outside with their candles, leaving the church in darkness. As midnight strikes, the cry goes up 'Christ is risen', and the people reply 'He is risen indeed.' They enter the dark, empty church like the first **disciples** coming to the tomb where Jesus had been laid to rest and finding it empty.

Sundays

This unit tells you why Sunday is a special day for Christians.

> **We sing songs to God and have a few prayers. The minister gives a talk. They read from the Bible, from the Old Testament and the New Testament.**
> – *Lisa*

People in church for a Sunday service.

What makes Sunday different?

Christians believe that Jesus rose from the dead on a **Sunday**, so Sunday is their **holy** day. It is a special day set apart each week for worship. Some Christians attend one **service** on a Sunday. Others spend most of the day on **church** activities. In the past, Sunday was a day of rest in Western countries. Now you can often find shops and entertainments open. Some Christians still keep Sunday special and different from the rest of the week. All the work around the house and garden is done on Saturday, so that there is time to relax on Sunday with family and church friends. People may dress up in nice clothes, which used to be kept for 'Sunday best'. The midday meal is traditionally the Sunday roast, the best meal of the week.

People dressed up for church.

Sunday services

A lot of churches have two services on a Sunday: one in the middle of the morning, and one at 6.30 in the evening. They usually last an hour. The services are a mixture of **hymns**, prayers, Bible readings and a **sermon**. About once a month there will also be a special service of **Holy Communion**. Some churches have Holy Communion Services more often than this. Many Catholics like to attend **Mass** every Sunday, so there are a number of services provided for them. These services usually last about 45 minutes. There might be one at 8am, 9.30am, 11.15am and 6 pm. Many Catholic churches also hold Mass on Saturday evenings for people who cannot get to church on Sundays, perhaps because of their work. Some churches have much longer services. If you go to an Eastern Orthodox Church, the service could well last for several hours.

Sunday schools

*Churches have to cater for all ages, and children may find the services rather long and boring if they are mainly for the grown-ups. So many churches run Sunday schools for children. Here they can worship God in a children's service and learn about **Christianity**. Sometimes children join in part of the main service, and spend the rest of the time on their own activities, led by Sunday school teachers.*

Children taking part in the church service.

Ascension and Pentecost

This unit tells you about the festivals that come after Easter in the church calendar.

> " **I think the Holy Spirit is the spirit of Jesus in the world. The Holy Spirit makes a difference to me, knowing that you've got somebody to look after you.** "
> – *John*

■ *An artist's idea of Jesus' ascension.*

Ascension Day

The Easter season in the church lasts for 40 days, and ends with **Ascension** Day. To ascend means to go up. Ascension Day is when **Christians** celebrate the end of Jesus' time on earth and his going up into **heaven**. People today no longer believe in a flat earth with the heavens above it, but we still speak of people going up. You might say you are going up a class at school. We might say someone is high and mighty, or that we feel on top of the world. On Ascension Day Christians celebrate because they believe that Jesus is now high and mighty, King of Kings, and at one with **God**. When he lived on earth he could only be in one place at a time. Now Christians all over the world believe that Jesus looks over them and hears them when they **pray**.

Pentecost

Ten days after Ascension Day, Christians celebrate **Pentecost**. It is also called Whit **Sunday**. Jesus promised his **disciples** that the Holy Spirit of God would give them power to preach about him to the ends of the earth. This happened at the Jewish feast of Pentecost.

'When the day of Pentecost came, all the believers were gathered together in one place. Suddenly there was a noise from the sky which sounded like a strong wind blowing, and it filled the whole house where they were sitting. Then they saw what looked like tongues of fire which spread out and touched each person there. They were all filled with the Holy Spirit ...'

The Spirit of God was said to be like wind and fire. This is because wind and fire are very powerful and are sources of energy. Wind and fire are used as symbols of the Holy Spirit, because the disciples were given power and energy at Pentecost to go out and preach about Jesus. Many people came to believe in him as their **Saviour** on that day. It was the beginning of the church.

Christians today pray that the Holy Spirit will give them power to do God's work in the world. Churches see the power of God working among them in different ways. Some claim amazing miracles of healing. Others feel God's spirit working quietly in their hearts, helping them to love and care for people.

How Pentecost is celebrated

The popular name for Pentecost is Whitsun, which comes from 'White Sunday'. It probably got this name because it was the custom for new Christians to be baptised on this day, wearing white. It is the third most important festival in the church after **Christmas** and Easter. In England the spring bank holiday used to be at Whitsun. It was the custom to go on Whit walks and picnics on the bank holiday Monday. In the North of England there would be Whit parades. In Derbyshire the parades often go to the local well, where there is a short **service** to thank God for the water. The wells are beautifully decorated for this occasion. Well dressing, as it is called, is done by building a wooden frame over or around the well. This is covered in damp clay and pictures are made by sticking natural things into the clay. All sorts of things can be used, like flowers, moss, shells, pebbles and seeds. They are usually religious pictures, showing scenes from the **Bible**.

Well dressing.

Harvest Festival

This unit talks about Harvest Festival, which celebrates the food and flowers that come from the earth.

> **We have our school's Harvest Festival at church. We bring in food for harvest. You can take anything. Last time, I took in some French soup and some custard.**
>
> – *Lisa*

Christians believe that **God** created the earth. At **Harvest** Festivals they thank God for all the good things that come from the earth.

When is Harvest Festival?

Some Harvest Festivals are held at the beginning of harvest time. In Scotland, Lammas is celebrated on 1 August. 'Lammas' means 'loaf mass'. A loaf of bread is made from the first wheat that is cut. It is taken to church for the bread which is eaten at **Mass**.

Some Harvest Festivals are held at the end of harvest time. In the Shetland Isles, in Scotland, deep-sea fishing used to end on 1 August. So they also gave thanks for the harvest of the sea at Lammas, when all the boats had returned safely with their catch of fish.

Autumn in the northern hemisphere comes between August and October. But it comes between March and May in the southern hemisphere. So this is when Christians in Australia and New Zealand celebrate their Harvest Festivals.

A church decorated for Harvest Festival.

How the harvest is celebrated

In Britain, churches often celebrate Harvest Festival in the autumn, when the wheat has been cut and the apples picked. The church is decorated with flowers and greenery. Fruit and vegetables are put on display, with a special loaf of bread in the middle. In some country churches a plough is brought in from a local farm. The **priest** says a blessing over it and **prays** for a good harvest in the year to come.

Why Harvest Festival is special

Harvest Festival reminds Christians of all the good things God gives them. This makes them want to share with others who are not so lucky. After the **service**, the food that has been put on display is usually made into parcels and given to people in need. Some churches make appeals for special things. St Botolph's Church in the East End of London collects things like soap, towels, tea and sugar. They give these to the many single homeless people in that area. They ask other churches in and around London to help them with this collection and stack everything up in the church.

harvest
APPEAL

ST BOTOLPH'S PROJECT
Working with people who are homeless

Please help St Botolph's Project in its work with homeless people by bringing:

- Coffee, Teabags & Sugar
- Tinned & Packet Soup
- Flour, Pasta & Rice
- Tinned Fruit & Vegetables
- Biscuits
- Tinned Meat & Fish
- Cleaning Materials
- Soap & Shampoo
- Automatic Washing Powder
- Shaving Foam & Disposable Razors
- Plastic Rubbish Sacks
- Towels & Tea Towels

St Botolph's Project
The Crypt Centre
Aldgate High Street
London EC3N 1AB
Tel: 071 283 1950/1670

A poster from St Botolph's Church in the East End, appealing for special Harvest gifts.

A priest at St Botolph's Church surrounded by the tinned food that has been given for Harvest.

Thanksgiving

This unit tells you how Americans celebrate Thanksgiving Day in November.

> **Since we've all grown up with pumpkin pie, it's a great favourite with us. But I made one and took it to school and none of the teachers liked it (except Gareth, who will eat anything). You line a pie tin with pastry and fill it with a mixture of pumpkin, salt, sugar, eggs, milk, and spices. It's baked for about an hour.**
> *– Anna*

An American teacher who works in another country tells us about the pumpkin pie she makes for Thanksgiving.

What is Thanksgiving?

Thanksgiving is one of the most important festivals in the USA. It comes on the fourth Thursday in November and is a national holiday. It celebrates the first **harvest** of the English settlers in America nearly 400 years ago. America was called the New World because it had only just been discovered by Europeans. These first settlers were Puritans. They liked to have a very simple, strict form of **Christianity**, based on the **Bible**. They went to America to start a new life and set up new **churches** where they could worship **God** in their own way.

These Mennonite Christians in Central America still live and dress like the early Puritans.

The Pilgrim Fathers

The journey across the Atlantic Ocean was very dangerous, but the Puritans made it. They called their settlement Plymouth. These first Puritan settlers are known as the **Pilgrim** Fathers and are honoured by Americans today as the founders of their nation. Over the next 20 years 20,000 more Puritans emigrated to North America.

Life was hard for the Pilgrim Fathers and almost half of them died in the first winter there. But they hunted for food and planted crops. The next year, when their first harvest was gathered in, they gave special thanks to God because it was proof that they could survive in this new land. This is the origin of Thanksgiving. It has been celebrated in America ever since.

How Thanksgiving Day is celebrated

On Thanksgiving Day many families attend Harvest Festival at church. They bring gifts to share with those who cannot afford to have a special meal. Big sports events are held. In some places there are parades, or the story of the Pilgrim Fathers is acted out.

Thanksgiving is a big family occasion. There is an enormous meal of turkey followed by sweet pumpkin pie for dessert. Roast turkey is traditional because the early settlers caught wild turkeys to eat. Pumpkins were grown by the early settlers and used both as a vegetable and dessert.

All Saints' Day and Day of the Dead

This unit tells you how holy people and Christians who have died are remembered in the church.

> **The saints – like St Mary and St George – are people that God chose to be special.**
> – *Lisa*

> **They have halos round their heads to make them look nice and peaceful and heavenly and special people.**
> – *James*

A statue of St Peter.

Hallowe'en

The evening before All Saints' Day is known as Hallowe'en. This is because 'hallowed' means holy or saintly; so 'all hallows' means 'all saints'.

Who are saints?

Saints are **holy Christians** who have lived their lives for **God**. This could be said of many Christians; but some churches have named particular people as saints.

St Peter was one of Jesus' 12 **disciples**. He became the leader of the church after Jesus died. In the statue above, he holds a large key. This is a symbol that he can let people into **heaven**. Peter made lots of mistakes when he was with Jesus, but Jesus forgave him and still chose him to be the leader. This shows us that saints are not all goody-goodies. They are people believed to be chosen by God to do something special for him.

Some Christians lead such saintly lives that people treat them like saints. Mother Teresa of Calcutta is one example. She has devoted her whole life to God and to the care of the poor who are sick and dying.

Saints' days

Many saints were **martyrs**. That means they died for being a Christian. That is why red is used in the church on saints' days. It stands for the blood of the martyrs. Often the saint's day, when the saint is remembered, is the day that he or she died.

All Saints' Day, on 1 November, is a chance for the church to celebrate all the saints. The **hymns** that are sung in church on this day often speak of the crowns that the saints wear. One hymn says:

O may we tread the sacred road
that saints and holy martyrs trod…
and win, like them, a crown of life.

This is a way of showing the Christian belief that the saints are rewarded with eternal life. For the same reason, saints are usually shown with a crown of light around their heads. This is called a **halo**.

Day of the Dead

The day after All Saints' Day is called All Souls' Day. It is when the church **prays** for Christians who have died. In Mexico it is called the Day of the Dead. It is a national 'fiesta' or festival. Skulls made of chocolate and icing are on sale everywhere. There are also cakes in the shape of skulls. People visit the graves of their loved ones who have died and put yellow flowers on them. Offerings for the souls of the dead are set out in public squares and in people's houses. They put out trays of bread, water, fruit and flowers. Many of these customs go back to the very old religion of Mexican Indians before they became **Christians**.

Mother Teresa of Calcutta.

Glossary

Advent the time of preparation before Christmas

Alleluia a shout of praise

altar table in a church used for Holy Communion

angel messenger from God

Ascension festival to celebrate the belief that Jesus reigns in heaven

Ash Wednesday the first day of Lent

Bethlehem the town where Jesus was born

Bible the Christian holy book

bishop a leader of the church

bless to make holy and happy

carol a religious song, usually sung at Christmas

chapel a church building, usually quite small

charity voluntary organisation to help the needy

Christian belonging to Christianity

Christianity the religion which follows Jesus Christ

Christingle an orange decorated for a special service; it means 'Christ-light'

Christmas festival to celebrate the birth of Jesus Christ

church group of Christians; also the building where they worship

David the greatest king of the Jews in Old Testament times

disciple a follower – for example, the 12 disciples of Jesus

Easter festival to celebrate the death and resurrection of Jesus

Epiphany festival to remember that Jesus was sent for the whole world

faith belief

fast to go without food

God the all-powerful, supreme being

Good Friday the day Jesus died

Gospel a type of book in the New Testament, about the life of Jesus

halo a circle of light around the head

harvest gathering in crops

heaven believed to be where God is and where people go after death

holy set apart for a religious purpose

Holy Communion the service which uses the symbols of bread and wine

Holy Week the week before Easter

hymn a religious song

Jerusalem the city where Jesus died

Lent the time of preparation before Easter

martyr someone who dies witnessing to their faith

Mary the mother of Jesus

Mass the service which uses bread and wine, also called Holy Communion

Maundy Thursday the night before Jesus died, when he ate the Last Supper with his disciples

minister a religious leader

Nativity birth

New Testament the last part of the Bible

Old Testament the first part of the Bible

Palm Sunday the Sunday before Easter Sunday; a festival to celebrate Jesus' final entry into Jerusalem

patron saint saint believed to protect a particular place or people

Pentecost the birthday of the church, when the Holy Spirit came upon the first Christians

pilgrim a religious person who travels to a holy place

Pope leader of the Roman Catholic Church, the bishop of Rome

pray to speak and listen to God

priest a religious leader

redeemer saviour, used to describe Jesus

resurrection rising from death

saints special, holy people

saviour someone who saves people, used to describe Jesus

sermon a religious talk

service an act of worship

Shrove Tuesday Pancake Day, the day before Lent starts

Stations of the Cross the 14 stages of Jesus' final journey on Good Friday

Sunday the Christian holy day each week

Further reading

World Religions: Christianity. John Logan; Wayland (Publishers) Ltd, 1995.

Religions through Festivals: Christianity. R.O. Hughes; Longman, 1989.

High Days and Holidays. David Self; Lion Publishing Ltd, 1993

Discovering Religions: Christianity. Sue Penney; Heinemann Publishers (Oxford) Ltd, 1995

Discovering Sacred Texts: The Christian Bible. ed. W. Owen Cole; Heinemann Publishers (Oxford) Ltd, 1994

Let's Celebrate Spring. Mike Rosen, ed. Deb Elliott; Wayland (Publishers) Ltd, 1994.

Let's Celebrate Summer. Mike Rosen, ed. Deb Elliott; Wayland (Publishers)Ltd, 1994.

Let's Celebrate Autumn. Mike Rosen, ed. Deb Elliott; Wayland (Publishers) Ltd, 1994.

Let's Celebrate Winter. Mike Rosen, ed. Deb Elliott; Wayland (Publishers) Ltd, 1994.

Understanding Religions: Food and Fasting. Deidre Burke, Wayland (Publishers) Ltd, 1992.

Understanding Religions: Pilgrimages and Journeys. Katherine Prior, Wayland (Publishers) Ltd, 1992.

A closer look

This picture shows a Palm Sunday procession in Latin America with a statue of Jesus on a donkey. Palm Sunday celebrates Jesus' arrival at Jerusalem for the Jewish festival of Passover. Jesus rode on a donkey to show that he came in peace. It is both a happy and sad occasion for Christians, for though they sing Jesus' praises, he died on a cross less than a week after he had entered Jerusalem.

Index

Plain numbers (3) refer to the text. Italic numbers (*3*) refer to a picture.